SEA LIFE CONTENTS

FISH

There are lots of kinds of fish. Fish are scaly-skinned, bony animals that swim in water and breathe using gills. Fish can be as big as a whale shark or as small as a clownfish.

Different fish eat different types of food. They can eat plants, insects, CRUSTACEANS and other fish. Bigger fish, such as sharks, also eat large animals, including mammals.

DID YOU KNOW?

To breathe, fish take water into their mouth and absorb oxygen as they push it out through their GILLS.

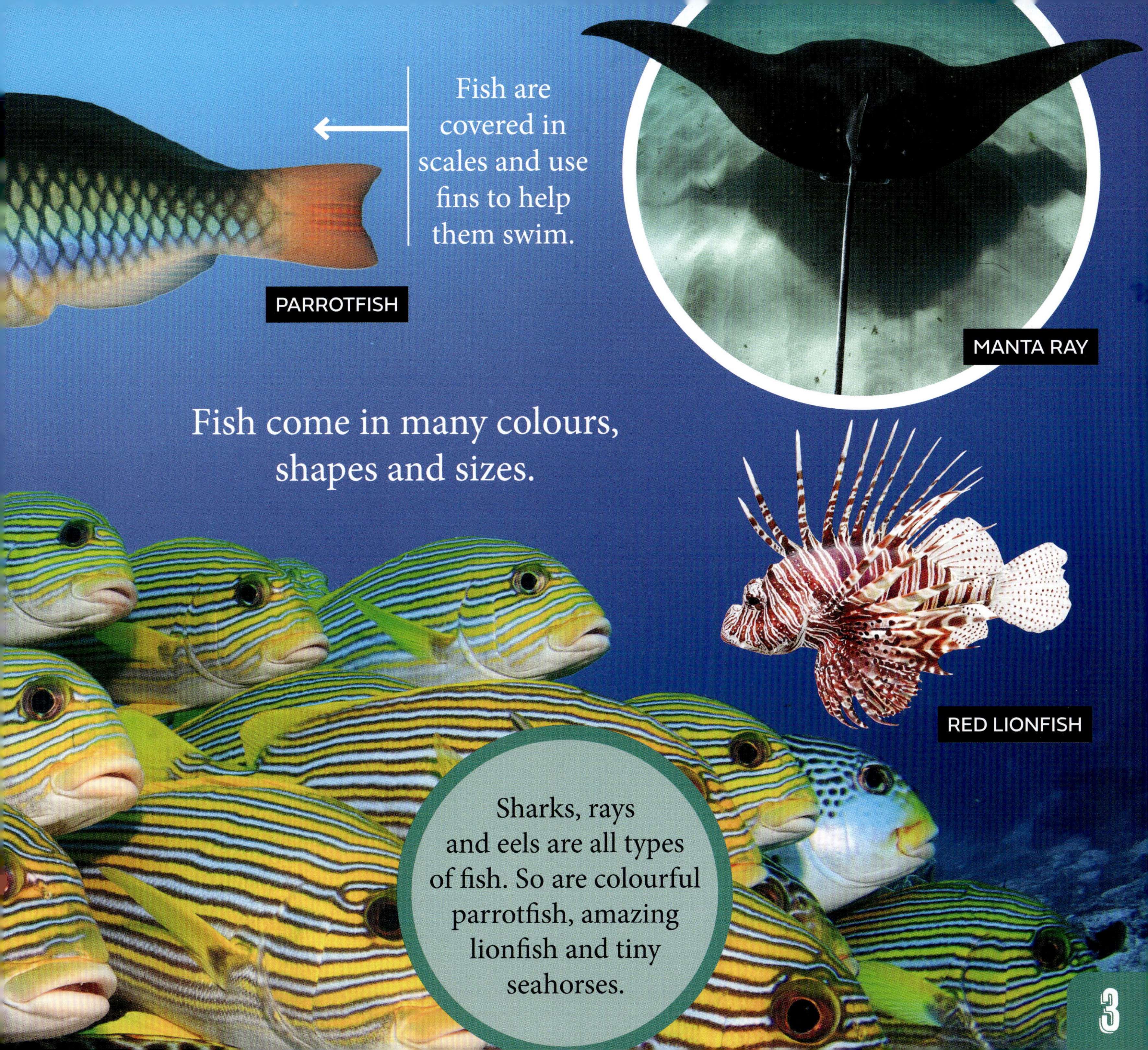
Fish are covered in scales and use fins to help them swim.
PARROTFISH
MANTA RAY
Fish come in many colours, shapes and sizes.
RED LIONFISH
Sharks, rays and eels are all types of fish. So are colourful parrotfish, amazing lionfish and tiny seahorses.

MAMMALS

Australia is home to many different marine mammals.

DID YOU KNOW?

All marine mammals have hair on their bodies but it is often hard to see.

Mammals that live underwater must come up to the surface to breathe air into their lungs.

Whales, dolphins, seals, porpoises, sea lions and dugongs are all sea mammals that can be found in our oceans.
DUGONG
HUMPBACK WHALE
NEW ZEALAND FUR SEAL
Like land mammals, mothers give birth to live young and make milk to feed their babies.

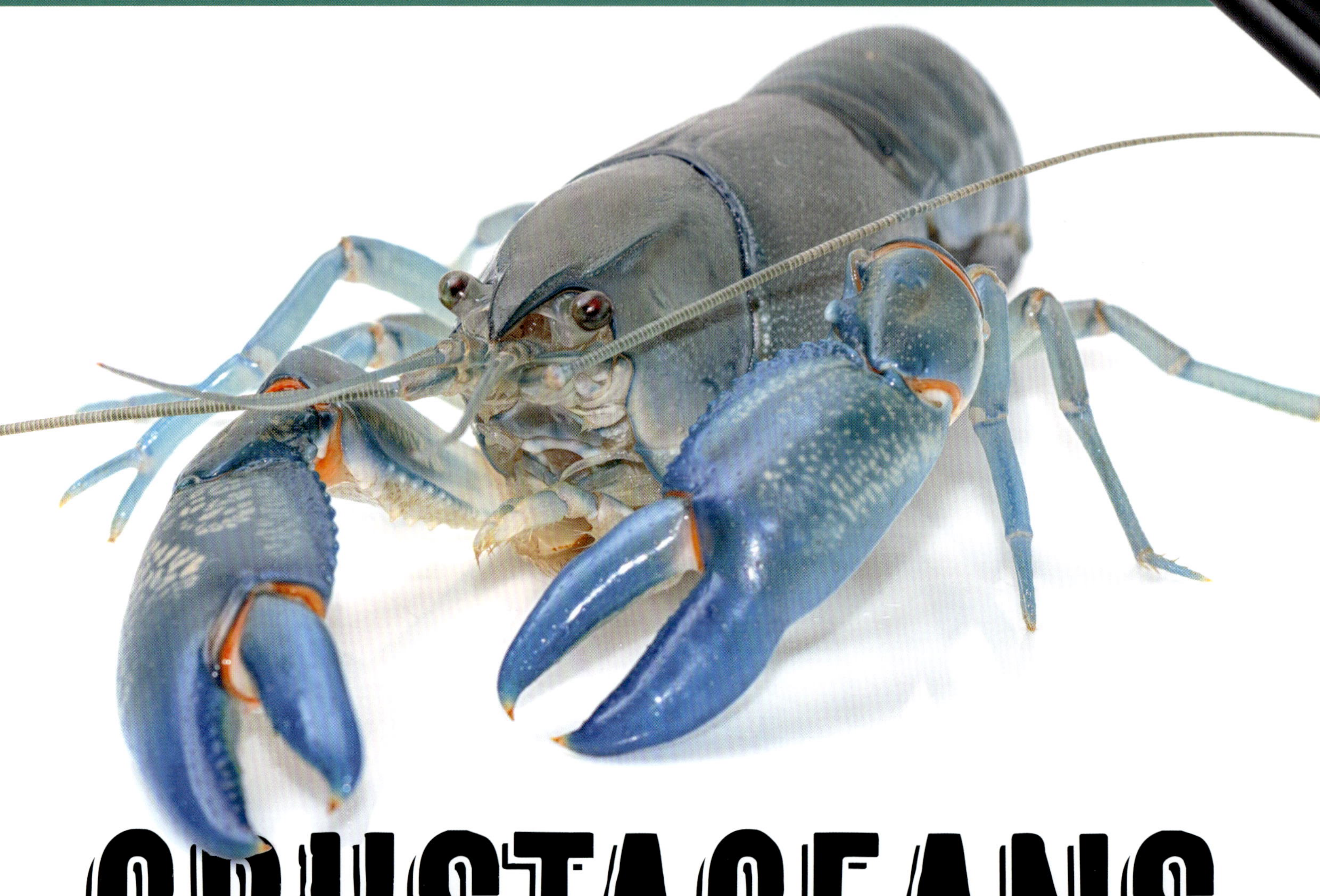

CRUSTACEANS

Crabs, lobsters, prawns and barnacles are all types of marine crustaceans.

DID YOU KNOW?

Crustaceans have hard shells. As they grow bigger, they shed their outer shell to make way for a new one.

Many crustaceans have powerful claws. They use their claws to protect themselves and to catch their food.

MOLLUSCS

There are many different types of molluscs in the ocean, such as clams, mussels, snails, sea slugs, octopuses and squids.

GIANT CLAM

Molluscs that don't have shells like to hide under rocks to avoid predators. Some of them, like the blue-ringed octopus, are also venomous and dangerous.

Molluscs have soft bodies with no bones. Many of them have a hard shell to protect themselves. These shells often wash up on our beaches, and some of them are very pretty.

MEET THE OCTOPUS

Learn all about this strange and beautiful sea creature.

They don't hear very well, but have very good eyesight.

SQUIRT!

Octopuses can squirt black ink to confuse animals that are trying to catch them.

Octopuses can taste what they touch using their suction cups.

The blue-ringed octopus is small, but some octopuses are large. The giant octopus, for example, is usually about 5m in length.

REPTILES

Australia's marine reptiles can be sorted into three groups: snakes, turtles and crocodiles.

Saltwater crocodiles live on the coast in Australia's north.

SALTWATER CROCODILE

DID YOU KNOW?
Saltwater crocs are the largest living reptiles in the world.

DID YOU KNOW?

When they grow up, female sea turtles return to the same beach where they hatched to lay their eggs.

FLATBACK TURTLE

HAWKSBILL SEA TURTLE

Six species of turtle visit Australian beaches. These are the green, hawksbill, loggerhead, flatback, olive ridley and leatherback turtles. All of our sea turtles are now endangered or threatened.

About 30 species of sea snake live in Australian waters. They have strong venom but rarely bite humans.

BANDED SEA SNAKE

SEABIRDS

Australia's seabirds are usually found near the coast. Sometimes they are also spotted inland, near lakes and wetlands.

ADÉLIE PENGUIN

DID YOU KNOW?
Penguins mainly live in Antarctica. Their black and white coats help camouflage them in the water.

One of our most common seabirds is the silver gull. It is a **SCAVENGER**, so it eats whatever it can find. If you're picnicking near the sea, you have to be careful or a silver gull might steal your lunch!

Penguins are another kind of seabird. Penguins can't fly but they are very good at swimming. They eat fish, squid and krill, which they catch in the water.

Other seabirds include terns, pelicans and albatrosses.

CORAL

They may look like plants, but corals are made up of many tiny animals called polyps. A large group of **CORAL POLYPS** is called a **COLONY**. Coral forms when each polyp in a colony builds a hard skeleton outside its body. These can be colourful, and come in interesting shapes.

Every year, coral polyps spawn and send out tiny bundles, called gametes. When the gametes join and settle on the sea floor, they grow into new corals.

When lots of hard corals make a giant colony, it becomes a coral reef. Coral reefs have existed on Earth for more than 200 million years. The Great Barrier Reef, in Queensland, is Australia's largest and best-known coral reef.

GREAT BARRIER REEF

DID YOU KNOW?

Coral turns white when it dies.

DAMSELFISH

Many fish use coral as a hiding place from predators. Some, like parrotfish, actually eat coral.

PLANTS

Marine plants use sunlight to help them grow, just like the plants that live on the land.

One kind of marine plant is seaweed. When lots of seaweed grows close together, it makes a kelp forest.

Mangrove trees grow in shallow areas along the coastline and riverbanks.
Fish and other sea creatures often eat marine plants. They can also live among them or hide from predators within their leaves or roots.
DUGONG
MANGROVE TREE
Seagrasses cover the ocean floor in some areas.

THE GREAT BARRIER REEF

The Great Barrier Reef is the largest living structure on Earth, made up of about 600 different types of corals of all different shapes, sizes and colours. Many animals, from microscopic **PLANKTON** to large humpback whales, can be found here.

The Great Barrier Reef is made up of coral. It formed millions of years ago in the Coral Sea, and most of it is located off the Queensland coast. It is more than 2600km long and can be seen from space. It is a World Heritage Site.

Visitors like to snorkel, dive or ride in glass bottom boats to look at the bright colours of the plants and animals.

The Great Barrier Reef faces many challenges today, including pollution and rising water temperatures as a result of climate change. These factors are causing coral to die, so it is important we take action to help the reef recover and survive.

SHELLS

Some sea creatures make and wear shells to keep them safe. Have you seen any of these?

TIGER COWRIE

The snail that lives in this shell crawls around rock pools all day and night. It looks pretty, but you have to be careful – this shell has very sharp edges.

GIANT CONCH

This shell is home to the world's biggest snail – the Australian trumpet, which can grow up to 91cm long. It lives in sandy, shallow water at the beach.

QUEEN FAN SCALLOP

Scallops are well known for being good to eat. Special fishermen dive down into the water to get them.

SCORPION CONCH

A snail that eats plants lives inside this seven-spined shell. At the bottom of the shell is a little peephole to see through.

SCALLOPED HAMMERHEAD SHARK

GREAT WHITE SHARK

SHARKS

Sharks have been swimming in our seas since before dinosaurs even existed. One kind of shark that lived up to 25 million years ago had teeth that were as big as your head!

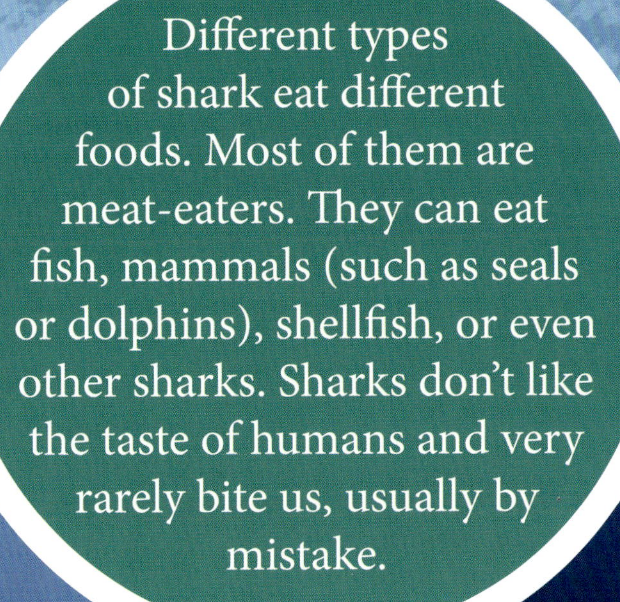

Different types of shark eat different foods. Most of them are meat-eaters. They can eat fish, mammals (such as seals or dolphins), shellfish, or even other sharks. Sharks don't like the taste of humans and very rarely bite us, usually by mistake.

Sharks have very powerful jaws and many rows of sharp, pointy teeth.

PORT JACKSON SHARK

Some sharks see very well, even in **MURKY** water, and they have an excellent sense of smell so they can easily hunt prey.

LIFE ON THE COAST

Canoes used to be made of bark, like this one from the Gubbi Gubbi people of south-eastern Queensland.

People living by the ocean have always collected food from the sea. Many Aboriginal communities were based by the coast. They would make canoes from trees to travel by water and hunt for food in bays, rivers and oceans. Today many people live by the coast and find food and resources in or by the water.

Traditionally, Aboriginal people living on the coast ate seafood, including fish, turtles and shellfish. They would put discarded shells in a big pile. These piles are called **MIDDENS** and many still exist today.

This is a midden. Can you see the shells on the ground? In a midden you might find shellfish and campfire remains, and the bones of fish, birds and sea mammals. There may also be tools made from stone, shells and bone.

Australians eat more than 350,000 tonnes of seafood a year!

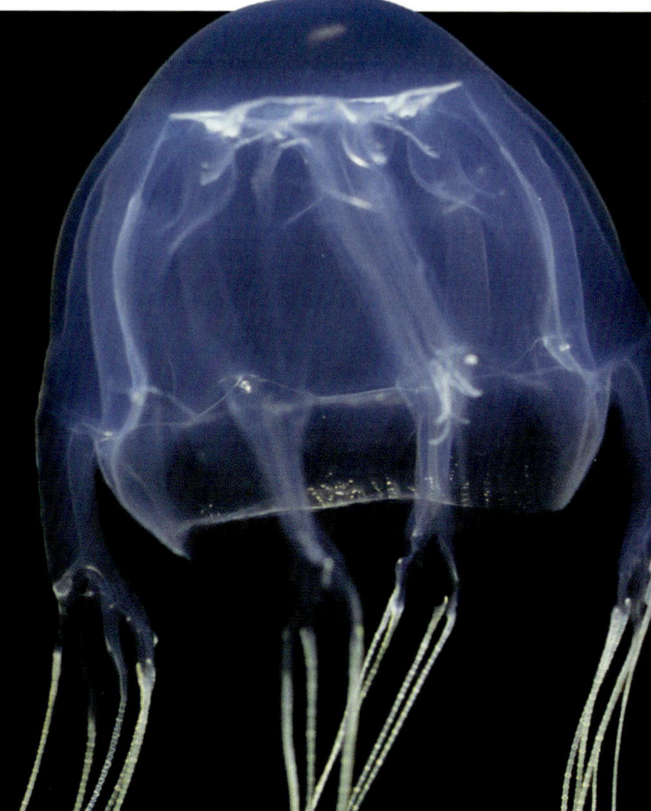

BOX JELLYFISH

All jellyfish sting their prey with venom, but not all jellyfish can harm humans. The most dangerous are the tiny irukandji and the box jellyfish. The box jellyfish has long tentacles that can reach up to 3m long and a powerful venom that can kill humans.

OLIVE SEA SNAKE

The olive sea snake lives in the ocean but comes to the surface to breathe about once every half an hour. It has toxic venom that it injects into its victims with its sharp fangs. It normally doesn't attack humans, but it may strike if frightened.

DANGER IN THE WATER

Some of them may look friendly, but you don't want to touch these creatures!

OLIVE SEA SNAKE

LIONFISH

The lionfish is a very pretty fish, but don't let that fool you! Its spines are venomous, and if it stings you, it will hurt a lot. Luckily, the venom isn't deadly for humans. If you leave the lionfish alone, it will usually stay away from you.

CONE SNAILS

Cone snails often have very beautiful shells, but you should never pick them up. They have tiny harpoons inside their shells, and when they feel threatened, they shoot these at their attacker. The harpoons sting a lot and can be poisonous to humans.

STONEFISH

A stonefish has 13 sharp, venomous spines on its back. It is one of the deadliest fish in the world. It rests on the sea floor to catch shrimp and fish. It blends into its environment so well that humans risk stepping on it and being stung.

GLOSSARY

CRUSTACEANS
Hard-shelled organisms that shed and replace their shells as they grow bigger.

GILLS
The part of a fish that lets them breathe.

MIDDEN
A pile of shells, bones and campfire remains that was left near the sea by Indigenous people who lived on the coast.

CORAL POLYPS
Tiny marine animals that settle in one spot with lots of other polyps and then form coral.

COLONY
A big group of coral polyps.

MURKY
Cloudy, foggy and difficult to see through.

PLANKTON
Very tiny plants and animals that float in the water and make up a shrimp's diet.

SCAVENGER
A type of animal that eats whatever food it can find.

PICTURE CREDITS

Images are listed clockwise from top left unless specified.

AG = Australian Geographic; SS = Shutterstock.com;

US = Unsplash.com; CP = CanvaPro

Front cover: Neirfy/SS; TENGLAO/SS; Ste Everington/SS; Kletr/SS; pistolseven/SS; TatjanaRittner/SS; Rich Carey/SS; Kotomiti Okuma/SS; Kotomiti Okuma/SS; Rich Carey/SS. **1:** Rich Carey/SS; Mark Spencer/AG; Kotomiti Okuma/SS; dive-hive/SS. **2:** Mark Spencer/AG; Rich Carey/SS. **3:** Justin Gilligan/AG; lakov Filimonov/SS. **4:** Schnapps2012/SS; Darren Jew/AG. **5:** Gudkov Andrey/SS; Alex Churilov/SS; Simon Carter/AG. **6:** Praisaeng/SS. **7:** JIANG HONGYAN/SS; Josef Szeles/SS; Jason Edwards/AG. **8:** Kevin Deacon/AG. **9:** Justin Gilligan/AG; Sascha Janson/SS; JPL Designs/SS. **10:** Vittorio Bruno/SS. **11:** Sahara Frost/SS; Fotokon/SS; YUSRAN ABDUL RAHMAN/SS; Rich Carey/SS. **12:** Vladimir Turkenich/SS **13:** Rich Carey/SS; Jiri Lochman/AG; Rich Carey/SS. **14:** Mike Rossi/AG. **15:** AnemStyle/SS; Radek94/SS; AndreAnita/SS. **16:** stockphoto-graf/SS; Mike McCoy/AG; Kevin Deacon/AG. **17:** Mike McCoy/AG; Mike McCoy/AG; Nick Rains/AG; Mike McCoy/AG. **18:** divedog/SS. **19:** Phil Lowe/SS; Damsea/SS; vkilikov/SS. **20:** Vlad61/SS. **21:** Nick Rains/AG; Tunatura/SS; Rich Carey/SS. **22:** Vlad61/SS. **23:** Mark Brandon/SS; Guillermo Guerao Serra/SS; Suriyawut_Khongyuen/SS. **24:** Alex Rush/SS; wildestanimal/SS. **25.** BW Folsom/SS; Craig Lambert Photography/SS; Tomas KotoucSS. **26:** Jimbo_Cymru/SS; Martin Valigurksy/SS; Don Fuchs/AG. **27:** Galexia/SS; Oliver Strewe/AG. **28:** Sahara Frost/SS; Nick Rains/AG. **29:** Indian Ocean Imagery/CP; Arthit Chamsat/SS; RobJ808/SS; Richard Whitcombe/SS. **30:** Andrew Gregory/AG; Marje Crosby-Fairall/AG; Seashell World/SS; arka38/SS. **31:** Aaronejbull87/SS.

Back cover: Richard Whitcombe/SS.

Australian Geographic

DISCOVER

Australian Geographic *Discover: Sea Life* is published by Australian Geographic.

First published in 2020, reprinted in 2023

52–54 Turner St, Redfern, NSW

editorial@ausgeo.com.au
australiangeographic.com.au

ISBN: 978-1-925847-76-5

Creative director: Mike Elliott
Editor Lauren Smith
Subeditors Rebecca Cotton, Peter Tuskan
Senior Designer: Harmony Southern
Print production: Andy Franks

AUSTRALIAN GEOGRAPHIC
Managing Director: David Haslingden
Licensing and Publishing Manager: Tom Bates
Commercial Assistant: Felicity McManus

Printed in China by C & C Offset Printing Co. Ltd.
The paper in this book is FSC ® certified. FSC ® promotes environmentally responsible, socially beneficial and economically viable management of the world's forests.

BOOKS IN THIS SERIES

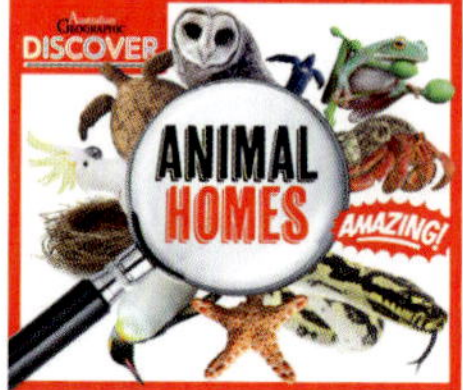

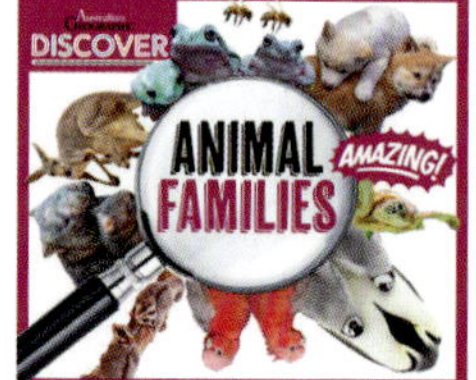

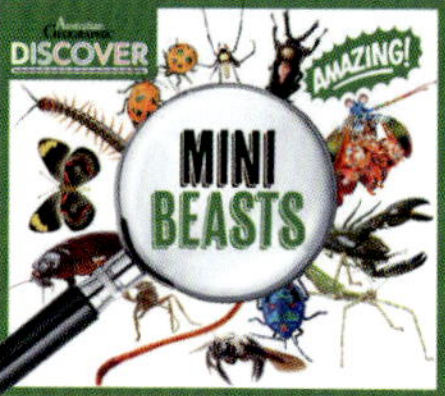

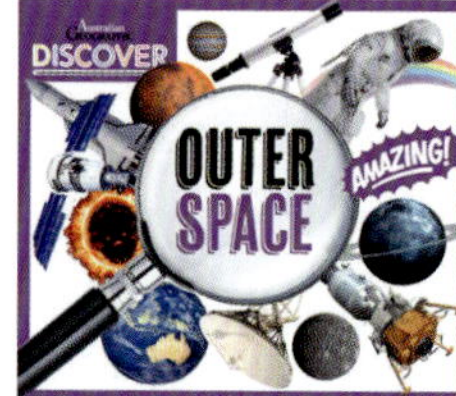

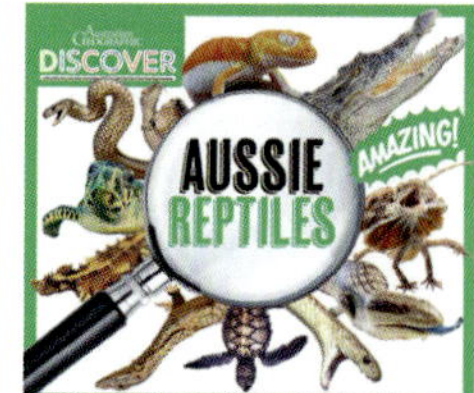

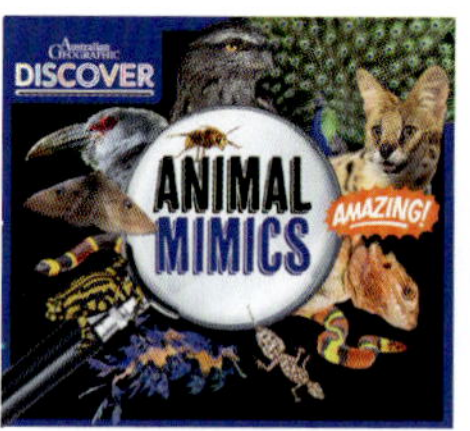

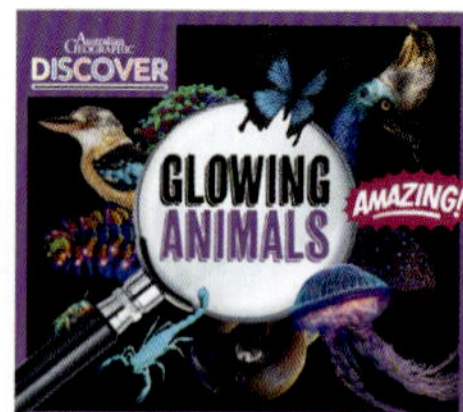

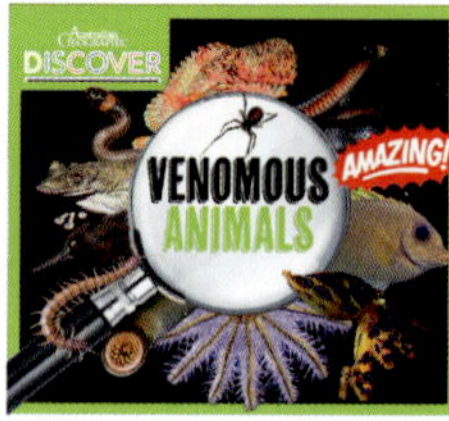

Australian Geographic contributes 100% of its profits to the Australian Geographic Society, including its conservation and sustainability programs.